DIUM
NG HOUSE
IELS STREET
I, NC 27605

se visit our Web site at
npublishing.com

lishing and its logo
d trademarks.

s Poetry
blen Edge

eblen Edge, 2020
s Reserved.

-944348-87-8

ER'S NOTE

ed on acid-free paper.

Dege's

Poetry

DEBLEN EDGE

PEN
PUBLISI
514-2O1 DA
RALEIC

For information, p
www.pena

PENDIUM P
are registe

Deg
By L

Copyright ©
All Rig

ISBN: 97

PUBLIS

This book is pri

Contents

BORROWED SMILES

Memories are borrowed smiles from someone else,

Just think of the smile on the face of an old friend after a long over due conversation with you,

Imagine the thankful look on someone's face when they say good morning and you smile back,

They needed that more than you did...

Enjoy the calmness of a customer when they hear the joy in your voice when you answer the phone,

And, treasure the contentment in the face of a child that tried something you suggested that really worked.

Then, wonder about the way you feel when you receive a compliment for being patient.

All of these events are smiles borrowed from someone else

Thanks for loaning me a smile!!!!

FREE INDEED

I am free, yes free
But am I still imprisoned?

Am I truly free?
Free Indeed
I can be anything I want to be
And, with the Father, The Son, and the Holy Ghost
I have everything I need
So, am I truly free?
Free indeed.

There are a people gone on before me
Their roads led them in many directions
One of them merged right into my many roads of life, and
It let's me look at and focus on their reflections

Reflections that connects me, a regular person to the history of
    this world
The reflection of the lady working in the big house – working
    and hungering for freedom
The reflections of a man in the fields – praying for freedom
The reflections of church holding service in a hiding place
So, am I truly free?
Free indeed.

The reflections of an underground railroad
The reflections of lynching of friends and family
The reflections of little girls being blown up in a church…. Yes,
    God's house of worship
The reflections of $2.99 PF Flyers and $200.00 Air Jordans

The reflections of that dorky kid Martin growing up to make a
    difference
The reflections of a history-making event—His birthday a
    National Holiday
So, am I free?
Free indeed

Again, I see reflections of children disrespecting themselves, their
    parents and me
The reflections of the house that is now affordable for our people
The reflections of myself in the mirror in the ladies' room at my
    good job
The reflections of the evolution of our people from slavery to
    prominent news, TV and government personalities
The reflections of me and the part I play in this evolution
So, am I truly free?
Free indeed
Did I stop and stand still?
Or, did I move on and make my stand
Am I truly free?
Free indeed....

REVIVAL

A gathering in the name of the Lord
A gathering to celebrate the Life of Christ
A gathering to learn the words of the Bible
A gathering to share with one another
A gathering to understand what we are suppose to do
A gathering to revive our spirit, lives, love and obedience
A gathering to remember:
    "Suffer little children and come unto me."
A gathering to have a revival
A gathering to honor the name of the Lord
A gathering to praise Jesus Christ
A gathering to revive our being
A revival to complete our essence
A revival is what we are having
A revival is what will guide us
And a revival this will be
Be brave and let's have a REVIVAL!!!

MOM'S TOOL KIT

Needles are used to mend holes
Tack on buttons and to stitch torn objects
Thread is used in conjunction with needles to hold the seams
    together
Witch stitchery is used to hem a garment and prevent it from
    being too long or dragging
Band aids to cover a bruise or scar to keep out infections
Scissors are used to disconnect and be finished, not done, but just
    finished

Now the real deal

Mom is the needle that mends the holes in our lives
She tacks on knowledge, and stitch love into our torn hearts
Mom takes threads of common sense, life experiences and faith
    in God to hold our seams together
She uses the witch stitchery of heart to heart talks, ego boosting,
    and faith in God so we won't linger long on the rough times
    in life or drag about feeling sorry for ourselves
Mom uses the band aids of hugs and kisses, her strength
    in God to ease the bruises of life's lessons, the scars of
    disappointments and to ward off infectious acts and thoughts
    that would prevent our hearts from being good
Scissors last but not least and of great importance
After Mom mends, tacks, stitches and bands our very essence
She gathers up the courage to clip that last thread that brings us
    to the present
For Mom knows her tool kit has served its purpose
Because, if you look around and then in the mirror, you can see
    Mom's handy work.
God Bless Mom.

THIS HERE CHURCH HOUSE

This here Church house
This here Church house is home
Been standing as long as I can remember
This building may have only been standing a few years, and gets
    rickety from time to time
But, the people in this Church house
Is what makes it a home, yes
This here Church house
This here Church house is home

The celebrations start with the first
Then go on to the second, third, and before you know a decade
    has gone by, and
Each year she sprinkles a little more seasonings upon us
It is for us to live within the right mixture
To grow more abundantly year after year, yes
This here Church house
This here Church house is home

This old building not long has it been standing, but
The people, oh no, let me correct myself
The Christians in this old Church house makes it home
Don't seem like a decade at all
'Cause this ole' rickety Church house been standing long as I can
    remember
This here Church house, yes
This here Church house is home.

This here Church house has housed slaves, the homeless, the
    sinful

This here Church house has made us convict ourselves and each other

This here Church house has fallen down around our ankles
This here Church house has held us together through slavery, wars, riots, racial situations, bombings of little girls in a church, our love ones being killed in unnecessary battles, births of new babies, snipers and especially our struggle to get closer to God

This here Church house has cried a many tears
This here Church house been keeping us together a long, long time
Don't seem like decades passed at all
'Cause this ole' rickety Church house been standing long as I can remember
This here Church house, yes
This here Church house is home.

VICTORY

Keeping strong the faith of our forefathers,
Being diligent with the wisdom taught,
Pursue the strength to continue on as the roads lead to victory.

Sounds easy enough???
Well, how strong is faith when life snatches the rug from
    underfoot, or
The bridge becomes a big hole,
Be strong in faith, Stand on faith
Before long there is a new and improved rug, a taller and shiner
    bridge,
Keep strong the faith, it leads to Victory.

Where is the wisdom that sturdies the road of life?
When the suffering, the tears and the bloodshed of forefathers
    long forgotten,
Where is the wisdom of knowing, helping they fellowman is the
    right thing to do?
But, taking the easy road choosing not to see or help is far from
    being cool.
Be thrift with wisdom, stay focused in wisdom be strong with
    wisdom
It leads to victory.

Where is faith and wisdom when the strength to go on and on
    needs a boost?
Where is perseverance when faith and wisdom decide to take a
    rest?
When walking through hard times, it's never alone
Help is there; the will to accept is not

When walking in faith, rugs may be snatched, bridges may
        become holes
All things in live may go wrong, but
Faith grows strong

Faith leads to possession of wisdom
The wisdom to continue to pray to feed faith
The wisdom of knowing when coupled with faith
It leads to victory

The only thing to do is go forward and claim the Victory,
Victory in Christ!!!!

A GIFT FROM GOD

Learning from the day of birth is guided by God's gift to children
    everywhere
God gave children a playmate
Someone that knows what's wrong before you can say it
Someone who has healing powers from God, and
Can ease from a broken heart to a skinned knee
Someone who has skin of silk and yet with
God's Grace and Mercy has skin tough enough to ward the devil
    off, because
Someone wears the whole armor of God.

Learning from the day of birth is guided by God's gift to children
    everywhere.
Big ones, little ones, old ones, young ones, babies and even in
    stages of senility
God's gift to you, me and children everywhere is
That great educator, the greatest nurse and skillful doctor in the
    world, the best chief, best clothes designer and lets not forget
    the most lovable and greatest hugger in the world.

I'm not talking about a star on TV
All these things fit the same person although different to you and I.

That someone is mother
She is a gift to children everywhere from God.

BEAUTY OF A FLOWER

You see her face every morning,
Hear her voice throughout the day,
    As she is soaking up the sunshine and the rain
She disburses it just right, bit by bit, to keep you growing
    As healthy as can be
She makes a beautiful day during a thunderstorm
She stretches wide her wings when you need to run into her arms
That shiver down your spine is when she is praying for you
She shares her wisdom with you that put schoolbooks to shame
She stays up late at night to stay ahead of your game
She works two jobs and cleans the house so you don't have to live
    in shame

This flower is a beautiful one
It is a colorful one
It stands strong against strong winds and heavy rains
This flower is a wonderful joy and is
No one other than Mother
The Essence of the most beautiful flower
I have ever seen
Thank You God for Mother.

NAKED AND NOT ASHAMED

From a child until the difference between right and wrong were
    made clear to me
I was naked and not ashamed
As time moved on sin became my cover and shield, my source.

God stepped in and showed me that profanity and bad attitude
    doesn't make me popular or a part of the in crowd
Jesus stopped by to say that self-righteousness is not the proper
    way to pretend to Praise God.
There is only room for one God.
Faith knocked on the door and I only cracked it because I could
    take care of myself, because I have faith in myself
Mercy kicked the door in slammed me against the wall
    proclaiming

Child,
God brought you here, although you never thanked him
I questioned, how so, Mercy began to remind me when I thought
    I was grown and was making grown folks decisions, and
    making them badly I might add
Who settled my mind and decision-making became easier and
    more productive,
Who opened doors of opportunity and suddenly success was at
    your feet, bills were paid,
Who wakes me every morning and,
Oh, don't forget who gave me food to eat and a loving family.

Grace was standing close by as I began to fade away and
    stepped in and started to guide my tongue, snatched my
    self-righteousness to its knees, then Grace reached around
    and brought Faith in front of me.

I grabbed onto Faith and begged for Faith to never leave me,
    because I cannot make this walk alone

For God to send Grace and Mercy to me
For Grace and Mercy to strip me of all my sinful cover
The veil has been lifted
And I know now the meaning of Naked and Not Ashamed

Naked of all the sins of the past
Naked of the stubbornness of not wanting to ask for forgiveness
    or saying Thank you.
Naked of trying to do as others wants done
Naked of the crutches that life makes so easy to get use too

Not ashamed to tell someone God touched me with a finger of
    love this morning
Not ashamed to proclaim Faith as my direct link to my Heavenly
    Father
Not ashamed to admit I can't do this on my own.
Not ashamed to declare that my life belongs to my Lord and
    Savior Jesus Christ

Naked and not ashamed to be saved.

IN MY FATHER'S FOOTSTEPS

Today is a day of celebration of Father's, but today I will call
them Dad
Today we acknowledge that Dad takes care of the family
He teaches right from wrong, and how to deal with life
Everyone is thankful for Dad

But there is a greater Dad, and today I will call him Father,
because
Without Him there would be no Dad

This Father healed the sick, made the blind see and the lame to
walk
This Father catches us just before we hit the bottom
He makes us turn right when we had intentions to go left
He takes us out of our homes to our neighbor to offer a help and
hand
This Father humbles and gives victory when the devil stands
against us
This Father tell us we are His own

Oh, to walk in my Father's footsteps is awesome
To be able to turn the other cheek
Give my neighbor the shirt off my back and food from my table
To know when Dad says he loves me and has my best interest at
heart, that he got his guidance from this Father
This Father takes away that blanket of hurt, anger and grief in
the heart
He places peace, contentment and salvation in the middle of the
most drastic crisis in our lives
This Father talks to our heart, He walks with us in trouble, and
He casts out our greatest fears

This Father gives understanding of life that has been taught by
    Dad
This Father makes Dad the man
So, I walk in my Dad's footsteps because he walks in the footsteps
    of this Heavenly Father

To walk in my Father's footsteps is awesome
Because, this Father makes Dad the man.

MY OFFERING

O – ONLY, F – FINDNG, F – FAITH, E – EVERLASTING,
   WITH, R – REAL
I – INSPIRIATION, WHILE, N – NEEDING NOTHING,
   BUT, G – GOD

Offering is it giving 10% of all your money
Is it giving all your worldly goods?
Is it being good to other people?

We pray for increase, we pray for enlarged territory
So, what do we offer as a trade?
Would you offer your trust in time of need?
Your love in loneliness
Wisdom in time of confusion
A hug and a hand in a fallen time of despair
Maybe a liver to someone on dialysis
Flowers on grandma grave
Put a kid through college
These are all the right things to do
These are all the things that are the makings of my offering

No, don't stop there:
Give to the devastated hurricane victims
Quit a good job and go to that location and be a volunteer
Buy Mom a new home, and
It still does not seem like it is enough.
So, let's start and begin again…MY OFFERING

A-Aggressive, B-Brave, C-Courageous, D-Diligent, E-Effective,
   F- Faithful
G-Giant, H-Hero, I-Inspiring

And it can go on and on, and still not be enough, now it's time to stop and really take a good look at…MY OFFERING

What we've done is still not enough
It is still not what is required…
What's required is to give of you.
But, you and I, we have done that already
We have given, we prayed, we were wise, strong and tender, we got larger territories and increased in every facet of life, and still not enough,
That's because it is not giving of you, it's helping others.

What's required from Our Lord, Our Savior, and Our Jesus Christ is
Give yourself, your heart, mind and soul all to Jesus

For it is He that wakes us everyday
He that clears the mind
He that opens the heart
He that determines what offerings we are to make, but first we must give
The ultimate, the one thing we don't have to shine it, we don't have to wash it, we don't have to dress it, we just have to give it…MY OFFERING…YOUR OFFERING

S-SUDDENLY
O-OUT OF THE BLUE
U-UNDER GOD'S GUIDANCE WE CAN
L-LIVE FOREVER

OFFERING…MY OFFERING-YOUR OFFERING…IS OUR SOUL!

A MOMENT WITHOUT THOUGHT

Life for most is simple, without thought,
We do our daily chores without a second thought,
Go to work, go to the grocery store, go to work,
All things of habit, we do it without thought.

We get up and get dressed without thought,
We lie down and go to sleep without thought,
The longer we do things without thought,
The harder God has to work to protect us.

A minute before work or stepping out to the grocery store, or
Even a moment in the morning before we attempt to get out of
bed would make things so much easier for our Savior.

Even a moment before stepping out to the store,
Even a moment when someone cuts us off in traffic,
Even a moment before we go to the kitchen to fix dinner,
Even a moment before we pick up the phone to answer or call
someone.

Even a moment to say, "THANK YOU JESUS".

Makes life even simpler once we think about it.

The simple phrase "THANK YOU JESUS"

Keeps life simple,

Without thought.

AN UNBREAKABLE CONNECTION

There is not a friend so faithful as you.
Except God. But
He's perfect so we'll not compare His faithfulness with that which
  we have.

When I needed:
  A shoulder to cry on, you were right there with those broad
  shoulders of yours, no matter how much you had on them
  you always had time to shuffle everything around and make
  room for me and my tears.

When I needed:
  Someone to listen to me baffle on and on about me and my
  problems, or what I thought were problems, you were there
  with both ears open wide to take in all I had to say and still
  you sat and nodded and let me figure it all out for myself.

When I needed:
  To check myself, or a stern hand or word from time to time
  you were right there again, just like a mirror image, just like
  that inner voice that makes you think twice, you were there.

It's true the few times you needed, and you sought to find me, I
tried to be there, just as strong, broad shouldered, and opened
eared for you as you were for me, and I'm satisfied that you were
pleased that I was there.

But...

For me the time and space on your shoulders, and eardrums you've had to replace was, is, and always will be a treasure in my life's hope chest of things I want to, need to remember in the future

    There is nowhere I can ever go,
    Nothing I can ever do, and
    Nothing I can ever say that will smear, or
    Tarnish the good and bad times we've been through, AND
    I will cherish what we have,   THAT
    Wonderfully Blessed Love from God…
    Forever and always.

A commitment that will never be broken!

FACE

The evening skies are blue
The bluest of blue that carries a sign of peace
Peace which comes with time,
And makes the whole world feel at ease.
The ease and comfort of living life with respect
The respect you can be proud of
Walk tall with respect and pride
Smile with ease and peace on your face.

The face reflects many things
Most beautiful of all is the pride that's shown there,
Tranquility can also be seen there
But if you don't have peace, all of it means nothing.
Therefore, look to the skies and find peace,
And show the true pride, respect and tranquility upon your face.

PROMISES AND BLESSINGS

We promised God that we would live right
We promised God that we would walk right
We promised God that we would pray right
We've broken our promise once or twice
He Blessed us anyway

We arose this morning with the chance to live right
We got kinda busy
But He Blessed us anyway
We got out of bed with the chance to walk right
We got kinda busy
But He Blessed us anyway
We started our day with the chance to pray for our lives
    And the things we have
We got kinda busy
But He Blessed us anyway

While we go through our daily travels and adventures
We see someone evicted or homeless on the corner trying to
    recoup
    Their life's interests
We think how lucky we are to have a roof, clothes and something
    to eat
We got kinda busy and forgot our promise and didn't thank Him
But He Blessed us anyway

God didn't promise us He would Bless us
And then get kinda busy and break His promise
Regardless of who calls on Him and what they need
He's never too busy to Bless us anyway.

THE DECTIVE

<u>M</u>ASTER <u>O</u>F <u>T</u>HE <u>H</u>OME <u>E</u>NTER <u>R</u>ESPECTFULLY

THAT'S MOTHER!

There is nothing she cannot see, hear or do.

Mother has a healing hand, and a soothing kiss.
Mother is soft
She is hard with tough love
Mother is God's light to the children of the world.

Mother is a radar detector – she can fine you in a crowd of a
     million.
Mother is a sleek detective – she can make you tell anything.
Mother is a jack-of-all-trades and a master of everything.

Mother, ma, mom is God's right hand.
Mother is a warm smile.
Mother is a stern look, a comforting hug.
Mother is a cure for ales.
Mother makes the boogieman go away.
She's in direct contact with the Master above, that's why she can
     say:

MASTER OF THE HOME ENTER RESPECTFULLY!

THAT'S MOTHER!

From Day After Yesterday Thru Day After Tomorrow

Day before yesterday we were babies,
Not aware that mother worked in the field by day and the big
    house by night,
Not aware that father worked the field by day and the barn by
    night, yet
We were feed well and were clothed with comfort by day and
    night.

Yesterday we helped in the field by day,
Tried to do homework by night,
Got out of school with grades earned by the blood, sweat and
    tears of the family.
We walked in peace movements,
We ran to save our own life,
We spoke out to show the world we were ready for the fight;
We survived the headscarf and rake era,
With a hoe and a cotton sack for accessories,
To the roaring twenties with shiny, shaky clothes,
And away from dem houses with no doors.

Today we are still climbing high on the shoulders of those gone
    on before,
Never minding about a house with no doors,
We are now proud owners of condos with multiple floors.

Tomorrow we'll stand in the shadows and observe our young,
Standing proud chest stuck out and all, while loudly proclaiming
"Lord just look at what you and me have done!!!"

Day before yesterday we began to learn,

Yesterday we were teachers,

Today we are history makers,

Tomorrow we'll have to step aside and let the younguns take
their turn,

Thinking of all the things, trials and tribulations that have come
to past,

T'was a long, long time ago, but oh my God how time really
went so fast.

For day after tomorrow they will be doctors, lawyers and
Presidents,

My oh my what a long way we've come from where we been
sent.

MY JEWEL

If I could explain what a sister is,
I would be rich,
The word sister and the person, is the most unexplainable in the
world,
Because a sister is a touch, a word of encouragement, a loving
shelter, a roaring storm, a tiger, a lamb and it goes on and
on.

What I do know and can explain,
She prayed powerful for me and you, and
She was always not far from reach
She's always rich in love, compassion and knowledge, and
Strong enough to never let me or you see her buckle under
pressure.
There was always a smile no matter how bleak the day or
situation.

In a sister there is always a pillar of strength and a couch to
God's own Grace
That songbird that God made to sooth the rough curves in my
and your life,
A sister is a precious gem, gift and a priceless jewel
A sister is a treasure that will never dull with age or time
She's my bright light in my life
And I thank God for her.

Rest now your work here is done.

FLOWERS FROM GOD

God's Flowers,
Oh, but God's Flowers
They are filled with beauty and fragrances of elegance,
They come equipped with words of encouragement,
They come armed with love overflowing,
They spread the positive power of Faith and prayer,
And, they embrace people everywhere.

They are songbirds of God,
Because they plant His knowledge and compassion,
They are strong and filled with grace,
Never a frown will be found on their face.

These flowers, of God's Children, be man, woman, boy, girl or
    infant,
Share their fragrances of life throughout the continents,
For His grace everlasting, to become
A treasure and so priceless they are,
For they emit the glow of truth and pride to all God's Children
    both near and far,
Thank You God for Your Children, thank you for the wisdom
    and the gumption to
Be that vase of fragrances, elegance and more
To step from Your Garden of Eden to earth's rugged floor
While blooming and blossoming forever more
With Your Beauty of Heaven a galore.

PRAISE YE

Our God is an Awesome God; Holy Is the Lamb; He's the Prince
of Peace

These are words to songs of Praise
Thus, Praise Ye the Lord

But, imagine this: A personal Praise
One that might go something like this:

The word PRAISE
Praise
Praise Ye
Praise Ye the
Praise Ye the Lord

P – Promise
R - Redeemer
A - Angel
I - Instructor
S - Savior
E - Energizer

His Promise is to love and keep us covered with protection from
harm and danger
He's a Redeemer, because He said, "Give me your sins and I'll
Redeem your Soul."
He's an Angel, for He is the Great I Am and the Angel of Mercy
to us all
He's an Instructor, for He teaches that the Truth will set you free,
therefore, living right is easy
He's a Savior...Jesus died so the Savior could live within us, and

He's an Energizer, because every time He shows His love for us it
    energizes our soul and heart

Therefore, we can't help but have a personal relationship with
    Him!

FOR THE PROMISED REEDEMED ANGEL INSTRUCTS
    THE SAVIOR TO ENGERIZE OUR SOUL...THUS

Praise
Praise Ye
Praise Ye the
Praise Ye the Lord
Praise Ye the Lord

Just Praise!!!

THANK YOU FOR THE SHIP

Lord thank You for our freedom
Lord thank You for our reason
Lord thank You for our low valleys
Lord thank You for our mountains we've climbed
Lord thank You for the passed days and time.

Lord thank You for the ship that landed that day
Lord thank You for all our ancestors it brought this way
Lord thank You for all the troubles they endured
For their lows are now our highs
Their hunger is now our fill
Their strength and faith help us climb life's difficult hills
Their brokenness is now our courage
Their journey and battle to be free
Keeps us in a closet walk with Thee
Their eyes resting on Your sparrow
Keeps our roads from being so narrow
The sweat on their brow
Lead to the opportunities we have here and now

Lord thank You for Harriett Tubman and Martin Luther King
    too
For they knew no one could exist without You
Lord thank You for sticking with them so thick
Cause You knew that today we might not be able to do the trick

Lord thank You for the ship that landed that day
For out of the humility and centuries of shame
Was born the days and times of a better way
With the world knowing that You are the coach of this game
Lord thank You for the ship that landed that day

And if we had to render an opinion, we would have it no other
    way
Because life has changed but yet stayed the same,
And we have so many riches all of them we can't claim
Lord thank You for the ship that landed that day, and now we
    know
Lord that You have the final say
Lord thank You for the ship that landed that day.

I Wish You Enough

I wish you enough sun to keep your attitude bright no matter
how grey the day may appear

I wish you enough rain to appreciate the sun even more

I wish you enough happiness to keep your spirit alive and
everlasting

I wish you enough pain so that even the smallest of joys in life
may appear bigger

I wish you enough to say thank you when you know you was
right and they were wrong

I wish you enough that when you fall with your basket of life's
eggs, nothing breaks

I wish you enough gain to satisfy your wanting

I wish you enough loss to appreciate all that you have

I wish you enough hellos to get you through the final good-byes

I wish you enough that you understand my bottomless thank you

I wish you enough that all your worries are as light as a feather

I wish you enough that 7762536 (problem) is the number you use
to call God

I wish you enough that you are in tune with Grace and Mercy

I wish you enough that your Blessing Cup is always overflowing

I wish you enough that you know I thank you, and

I wish you enough that your joy grows more and more each day
and year

I wish you enough that you know that you are appreciated, and

I wish you enough that our bond cripples all evil because of our
love, and

I wish you enough love that you glow every morning you wake
with the touch of an angel.

GOD KNOWS

No matter how far and wide the river flows,
When all things are done for our best,
God is the only one who truly knows,
The appropriate time for us to take our rest,
My dear, your days on this earth have come to an end,
But I know you are with your one and only true friend
Your life here was filled with all sorts of rewards,
As we sit with tears in our eyes,
We may be sad and will miss you dearly.
Without question we know you have come into your great
      inheritance and true prize.
Because, I feel your smile as you are looking upon the one who
      clearly knows, that
Now you must rest my love,
For your troubles are over,
Just whisper to Jesus you are glad to be there.
Then kindly ask if you can save us all a chair.
Be still and rest now,
Because you are finally with the Best.

I Pray for You

Today I pray for God to be with you,
Today I ask God to protect you,
Today I ask God to hold you,
Today I pray for your understanding,
Today I say to you God is in control,
Today I know God sees and is holding your heart,
Today I feel how you feel, because I had a family member not
    long out of the arms of danger,
Today I know that no matter what we think God is there and
    holding everything up,
Today I know God will give you the Blessing of your heart,
Today I know that He will let us know when He decides to call us
    to rest, but
If I may be so bold,
Today I feel it is not that day.
Today I pray that I am a cool calm voice for you, and
Today I pray for your strength, courage, contentment and faith
That God does all things good and according to HIS Will.
Today I give myself in prayer for you and your family.
God Be With You.

The Other Side of the Train

I see buildings, highways and byways and train tracks
Not bad scenes, but
Not the wonder of the duck in the stream
The trees are still resting from the winter's shedding
Patches of brown grass looking golden in the sunlight
Oh what another wonderful day
God has made.

The coldness and windiness of the day
Brings warm feelings and thoughts of God's Glory
For because of Him I am alive
Because of Him I have love in my heart
Because of Him I can be a testimony to a stranger
Because of Him I write
Because of Him I believe
Because of Him I will succeed.

My Fellow Veteran

Dedicated to all who served in war and peace:

Sitting on a hill, in a foxhole or behind a tree,
I decided to have a conversation between me and Thee.
My buddy and I looked across at each other,
I know that's my buddy from another mother.
We jump and move together back to back,
At the rifle bullets first tone,
Then I whisper, Thank You Lord
You didn't leave us here alone.
As things quiet down and the air is still,
I whisper again, Lord thank you we're still on this hill.
The dotted line I signed not so long ago,
I wonder what, was I thinking, why didn't I know,
Whilest I sit out in the hot summer or wintery snow,
Does anyone back home really know?
What we push through for our country to stay together,
And it is not the makings of a picture show.
As I close this conversation, I want to take a minute
To ask for Your blessings, Your grace and mercy for those of us
    out here in dangers way.
And for my buddies on this hill, in this foxhole and behind this
    tree,
I give thanks to You for Your loving blanket of protection around
    my buddies and me.
As we proudly serve for our country each and everyday because
    of Thee.

I salute you my friends, fellow Veterans and Buddies be blessed.

PRECIOUS GOLD

As a river flows freely,
So does smiles, hugs and love.
As bonds and ties shine bright,
So does this family in God's sight.
While we toil and labor through the day
So does our riches we share in every way.
As our hearts are connected in God's fold,
We know we have each other
Till we grow pleasantly old.
The sisterhood we have is a precious gift I am told,
Therefore, you are my personal piece of gold.
We are one you see, yet each one of a kind,
A more successful family no one will ever find.
Because, as we move forward, we leave none behind,
For each day at one point or another you are on my mind
And the thoughts of this family is never a waste of time
Today let this be said so that you will know
You will be carried in my heart where ever I go.
To be exact God is in you as He is in me
That is a family connection that will always be.

SUNSHINE

Sunshine is bright,
That is you…
Sunshine is warm,
That is you…
Sunshine brightens a gloomy day,
That is you…
Sunshine and a bright day
Chases all cares away,
Sunshine after the rain,
Brings nature alive again.
Sunshine is ever present,
Even on a cloudy day,
Sunshine peeks through all the madness along the way,
Sunshine is the best part of any God given day,
Sunshine, that is you…
Regardless of what you feel or what you say…
Sunshine, you have just brightened this day!!

Who We Call

We call on JESUS, LORD and GOD then we step away from
SIN,
But
Have we really stopped to think what all these words mean?
Let's take a stab and see what we get:

J – JUST
E – ENOUGH
S – SALVATION TO BE
U – UNMOVABLE FOR YOU MY
S – SAVIOR
L – LOVE
O – OVER
R – RAFT, AND
D – DECEIPT

G – GUESS WE
O- OWE YOU MANY
D – DEBITS

S – STOP
I – IGNORING
N – NEW FREEDOM IN JESUS, LORD AND GOD

NOW THAT WE HAVE MEANING
WHAT SHOULD WE DO

THANK YOU, JESUS

Streams that wind and bend through a city are
Like the events that filter and flow through life
Some flow to a dead end and just sit and fester bad things
Some start large and as they flow, they get smaller and smaller
    until it's just a thin line through the cracks in the sidewalk
Others start small, get large, then narrow and small again, and
    even smaller still but they keep flowing with determination

Such as life it flows like streams
Sometimes flowing to a dead end,
Sometimes to a small thin line barely noticeable
Then life can start small, get large then narrow down and get
    smaller but keeps on flowing

Just remember no matter
If your flow is slow, just keep flowing
If your light is dim, just keep shining
If your stream is almost gone, just be determined
If you're falling, just fall
There is someone that no matter what the status is
He will make life's slow flow become swift,
Dim light be the brightest ever, and
Thicken the volume of that almost gone stream
Just fall He will never let you hit the bottom
(we put ourselves there)

It all comes to just saying three words
When the evilness of the day steps up, just say three words
When Satan decided to step in the light, just say three words
These words are more powerful than anyone realizes,
Just think when saying these three words

The flow is still flowing even if slow,
The light is still shining even if dim and
The fall was real, and the bottom never came,
and for all of this we call His name,
THANK YOU, JESUS

DANCE LIKE DAVID DANCED

Today God smiled and woke the world
Today He reminded us we needed nothing but His Love
Today we have been Blessed by His graces
We are in the same shoes as David
Remember him? He was a favored child of God.

There is a song that goes like this:
It is getting hot in here, makes me wanna take my clothes of
Hot in here, hot in here

Let's just imagine that this one particular day
David heard this song in his head and began to dance
And dance to thank and praise God

According to the Bible, David danced out of his clothes
He danced out of his woes
He was a man after God's own heart
So, he prayed and danced even before his Blessing would start

David just danced, danced and danced some more
For all Blessing David danced
For each Blessing separately David danced
For Grace and Mercy for others David danced

Dance every day for you gift of Life
Dance in every way for the Blessings God sends you
Dance from your heart to show humbleness and gratitude
Dance, dance, dance like David danced

Remember it is not the dance, but
Who you are dancing for,
Today God smiled and woke the world
We were included and we should dance
Today we received God's Love and we should dance
Today He Blessed us all with His Graces and we should dance
We may not dance like David today, but
If we keep dancing with praise and praise dancing
We WILL be able to dance like David danced for the Love of
    God.

LEAD ME TO VICTORY

Keeping strong that faith of our forefathers,
Being diligent with the wisdom taught,
Pursue the strength to continue on as the roads lead to victory.

Sounds easy enough???
Well, My Sisters and Brothers, how strong is that faith when life
    snatches the rug from under foot, or
That bridge becomes a big hole,
Be strong in faith, Stand on faith
Before long there is a new and improved rug, a taller and shiner
    bridge, and
So my Sisters and Brothers,
Keep strong that faith, it leads to Victory.

Where is the wisdom that sturdies the road of life?
When the suffering, the tears and the bloodshed of forefathers
    are long forgotten,
Where is the wisdom of knowing, helping they fellowman is the
    right thing to do?
But, taking the easy road choosing not to see or help our
    fellowman is far from cool
Be thrifty with wisdom, stay focused in wisdom, be strong with
    wisdom
It leads to victory.

Where is that faith and wisdom when the strength to go on and
    on needs a boost?
Where is perseverance when faith and wisdom decide to take a
    rest?

When walking through hard times and it's seems like you are all
     alone,
Help is there; the will to accept is all gone,
When walking in faith, rugs may be snatched, bridges may
     become holes
All things in life may go wrong, but somehow
That Faith continues to grow strong.

My Brothers and Sisters,
Faith leads to the possession of wisdom
The wisdom to continue to constantly pray, feeds that faith
The wisdom of knowing, when and coupled with faith
Leads to victory.

The only thing to do is go forward and claim the Victory,
Victory of that strength we hold, we share and build upon,
Victory my Sisters and Brothers through the strength we get from
     Christ!!!!

STRONG SASSY SISTER CHALLENGE

Be my sister and be sassy enough and strong enough to be honest with me.

Be strong enough in a very sassy way to tell me to check my attitude.

Be sassy enough to strongly say to me, "that man is using you and he's not the one."

Be my sister and hug me and pray with and for me when I'm going through.

Be strong enough to sisterly teach and guide me when I have strayed off the right path.

Be my strong sassy sister and call me out when I'm wrong, and

Be that same strong sassy sister grown enough to receive the same.

Be that strong sassy sister to compliment me honestly when I'm right and when I look good.

Be my strong sassy sister and challenge me to become better, not bitter.

Be that strong sassy sister to be a good friend and always have my back.

Be that sister that will encourage me, push and hold me up when I'm falling.

Be that strong sassy sister grown enough to receive the same.

Be my sassy strong sister because - I am your strong sassy sister!

FROM WITHIN

A castle is not the only house for us as Queens

A three-story house or condo is not the only home for us as
    Queens

Washington DC, Denver, Clinton or Woodbridge is not the only
    cities for us as Queens

This room is not the only room for us as Queens

The only place for us as Queens, that we all know so well, is from
    Within, For

From within we shine with knowledge

From within we glow of courage

From within we emit warm rays of love

 From within we are as steadfast as stone walls

From within we illuminate a room upon our entrance

From within we help our sisters carry the load

From within we cascade reason and truth for easy access of our
    loved ones

From within we display all the nurturing, love, strength and
    respect to, for and of our fellow Daughters

So, from within: every time you walk into a room or look into a
    mirror

Do it from within for there you will find the true birth of a
    Queen

So, my Queen be victorious from within.

If you could imagine what Your Love one's last thoughts would have been, I think they may have gone something like this: The Great I Am has asked me to pass you this message:

CHANGING TRAINS

I must step briskly the train is about to leave and I can't be late,
    because
I'm changing trains,
Moving to a new neighborhood,
One where I can spread my wings even wider than before,
I'm changing trains!

My wingspan has been wonderful, full of activities and fun.
But I have to change trains,
In life my wings were a little unsteady at first, but
As I grew my wings got stronger and stronger, and God blessed
    me, because
I became a bonded with family and friends,
Oh, my goodness…WHAT A JOY…!
But I have to change trains.

Now, after many ups and downs and being grown, with long
    roads traveled,
I knew I was never alone,
I never quit for I had to care for my family and home,
I did not panic because God taught me how to move on,
It may have gotten a little shaky, but Jesus never let me unravel,
Now my road has been shortened of all my travels,
So…. I have to change trains.

I rode the highway of life for so many years,
I have been many places, met many people,
Learned a lot of things, and now the time has come to close the
final station,
And, it is also time to change trains and move on to something
new and improved.

Family, I love you dearly, but
I have a call from another so clearly,
I know it must be difficult, but a call I must answer surely,
because
I'm changing trains…

I must step briskly, the train is about to leave, and I can't be late,
because
I'm changing trains…

This train I am about to board, will be the best yet, because it
will be
Blessed by the Lord,
Conducted by Jesus,
Protected by Angels,
And, don't you worry,
THIS TEAM HAS GOT MY BACK!!

I must step briskly now, because the train is about to leave,
And I don't want to be late, because
I have to change trains.

BE BLESSED, AND REMEMBER I'LL ALWAYS BE IN YOUR HEART.

FRIEND

A friend is a word that has a great meaning,
Even though friends are far and few in between to be found,
But, once a friend is found, .
The meaning of the word itself begins to blossom through.

A kind word, a nice gesture
That's what a friend is,
Experiencing ups and downs together
That's what a friend is.

As time goes on and we all get older,
I've found very few people that are real friends to me.
So smile when you find a true friend,
Because it will be a long time before,
God will be that good to you again.

You Have A Friend In Me, Do I Have A Friend In You?

I AM YOU

You ask who am I
I am a nice, kind, loving woman after God's own heart
You ask who am I
I am a mother, wife, daughter
I can be one or all at any given time
You ask who am I
I am a supervisor, subordinate, or coworker
I plan, organize, fix things, cook and pump gas
I can get up at the crack of Dawn after going to bed 10 minutes
    prior, and
Still be fresh minded and beautiful

I am the one who has you in my heart and you don't know it
I have you on my mind and I call you to show it
I am your sister
I am your alter ego
I am your friend
I am your string that never breaks

Sunshine is my smile for your everyday peace
Pride is my character for your travels of this world
Successful is my wish for this life you hold from God

You ask who am I
I am that dot that connects me to you my sister and you my sister
    to another sister,
When the circle is finally complete it comes back to my
    connection to you my sister,
Because you ask who am I, well
I am you, you are me and we are one.

THE SILENT AND THE PURE

As the stars and moon light the skies at night.
Your warm smile and humble heart,
Make our world much more bright.
The warm helpful hands you always offer,
Places a touch of perfection that makes everything alright.
People say and think you are shy and quiet,
But, if we just take a second look,
The shyness in you is God speaking through your work,
The quiet we see is the calm as we learn from your strength as
    you pass it on.
For the care and attention you have showered upon us,
It is now our time to show love and gratitude to the silent and the
    pure.
You have shared your wisdom, and
Seasoned us with your strength, now
We package it all together and pass it back to you,
Filled with love and gratefulness of your steadfast years of service
    to us.
And with that same love we leave you with this:
Proverbs 30:5
"Every word of God is pure:
    He is a shield unto them that put their trust in Him."
Continue to be His silent and pure soldier.

WRITTEN
FOR
MOM

A STRONG GRAIN OF LIFE AND LOVE

From the days of getting started
To the days of being fruitful
A grain can produce many beautiful things
A flower, a fruit, a tree, a blade of grass and a new generation.

Our ancestors worked hard to get things started
The grain they sewed produced order, self-esteem and stamina
They taught us beliefs that are strong
Belief in God, which makes life long
Beliefs in ourselves so that we know that with God we can do no
    wrong.

A grain builds and grows beautiful structures
Look at Adam and Eve, they were
An existence from a grain
We exit from a grain
A grain of enthusiasm
A grain of determinedness
A grain of hope
A grain to guide through the wrong ways
A grain to cheer through the right ways
A grain of survival in every day.

Their ideas and guidance are the flowers from a grain
Their life was a tree from a grain
We are fruits from a grain
All things beginning with a grain
I have a grain, you have a grain
Putting them together we are the products of,
The Lord God Almighty

A grain that produced fruits, flowers, blades of grass and new
    generations
Where will our grain settle, a question we ask
Isn't it awesome what we are Gifted with, a grain for all to
    behold!
They planted your grain and blade of grass,
Making sure our grain will stand fast, while
Looking at us and our generation they were
Making sure it would surely last.

YOU ARE A BLESSING

I sat to pen a thank you note to you.
I sat with tears in my eyes for how God blessed me through you.
I sat thinking that thank you was not enough to say.
I sat wondering how I would ever repay you.
I sat knowing you don't want payment.
I sat joyfully knowing that you obedient to God's will.
I sat feeling God's love illuminate from you.
I sat smiling for I know you are true.
I sat claiming that we are connected.
I sat listening for God's words to come to me for you.
I sat and heard His words so this I deliver to you.
Dear friend my heart is filled with pride to know you.
My heart is overloaded with true sisterly love.
I am grateful because God placed you in my life.
And, in His name we are true friends now and always.
With all the love a sister can muster, I thank you and love you.
My prayer is that God continues His blessings upon you and
    grant the desires of your heart forever.
With a true sister bond, I love you.

DON'T COMPLAIN

If you didn't vote
Then don't complain
If you didn't vote for Obama
Then hush up and handle your pain
If you are not on board with change
Then don't expect your life to be rearranged
If you can't believe that is a Black President
Then the faith and love in you has be carelessly spent
If you didn't vote
Then don't complain, because
This 44th President being Black is by God so ordained
By God this has been ordained
So goes the burden of another strain
Lift up your head and shoulder the life of change
Step smartly on faith and strength
Contribute to the task at hand, because
If you didn't vote
Then don't complain.

44TH INAUGURAL CEREMONY

A PRAYER

Life is hard and sometimes unfair, but we know that Faith keeps
   us here
God will never put anything on us that we can't bear.
So, we take the time to always say a prayer
I pray that this you know, when God blesses you,
You will grow, your heart will feel and know,
God is the one and only shining light in your life that makes
   things so true.
I am here to say, when all else fails and when there is no one
   around, remember,
Forward all your issues to Heaven, for the line is always open,
   because
Jesus paid the price to discount our cost, and that He always got
   our cover… yes He is the boss.
He shows us all that our short-changed loss is not the ultimate
   value of our cost.
That we are more valuable to Him than our short-changed
   thought,
As we always put our Faith in Him who is the I Am that lights
   our path,
There is no question that our family ties will forever last.
So, forward your issues to Heaven, and
Always say a prayer, for surely
All your answers you will find there.

I AM YOUR FRIEND

Of the many things in the world,
A friend is highly treasured.
A friend is priceless.
When life has a hole in it,
A friend is space filler.
When the need for comfort creeps in,
A friend somehow knows when to appear.
When the need for encouragement, and trust arise,
A friend is always near and seems to be very wise.
You can argue, fuss, complain and even dismiss,
But, a friend is so steadfast that they will ask, is that the end of
      your list?
A friend is an extension of the meaning of supporter.
Do unto others as you would have them do unto you,
Once you have a friend, place that friend on a special shelf,
      because
No one knows you better than yourself, except for a friend.
No one will stick with you to the very end, except for a friend.
Be it mom, sister, brother, stranger or some other kin,
You can still consider them your friend.
I am here today to tell you I am your other kin!
And I will tell anyone and everybody: I AM YOUR FRIEND!!

Love from My Heart

She whom God gave me, I now give back.

She whom God blessed me with, I shared her, and we blessed others

She whom God granted us things to do together, we helped others

As the old saying goes, when God sees your work, He presents Angle wings according to the words of an old gospel song "May the work I have done speak for me."

God heard you and decided you were at a resting stage in your life and He decided to call you home to rest with Him and presented you with your wings.

Now, I say to you, the work you did really speaks for you.

All the family has been blessed by you, through you and because of you.

God loaned you to us for a little while and now you have the best gift of all,

You are home with the Lord.

Tarry no more Mother, because now it is time to rest my love for you are truly home.

I will miss you, but I know you are with one greater than us all and you are at peace.

I wish to say to you now, I'll see you on the other side one day and I pray you enjoy your peace.

I will always treasure you, along with all the love that flowed from you to me,

But now you must rest dear one for I see one set of footprints in the sand, and now know

You are ultimately blessed.

For someone whose Mother is in Heaven

A Clear Passage

You have binded our hearts,
Entwined our lives,
Taught us love, honor and respect
Touched us with smiles, interest and sound judgment.

Sound judgment to know that God makes no mistakes,
Interest to realize we must share your teachings with others,
Honor that we continue to make you proud,
Respect to live and show the light you sparked in us,
Smiles to let others know and see that,
Today we must move on with courage and understanding of,
Your ingredients of love, honor, respect, judgment and smiles.

For this we thank God for letting you pass our way,
For this we love you,
For this we will truly miss you.

Now we see one set of footprints,
Enjoy the ride for you are home
In the arms of God!

YOUR LOVING FAMILY

The Rain

The rain seems to show the day a love one transitions
Even more common it rains the day before
The day of transition
The day after or all during this process of transition to the very
    end
This happens for a reason
Rain is God's liquid sunshine mixed with His tears.
His liquid sunshine and tears cleans the air
Which paves a pure road for our love one to follow
His tears mixes with our tears so that we will know
He realize that we hurt, but
He needed for our love one to be free from pain
For this He sends the rain to wash away our pain and turn it into
    joy
For now our loved one is at rest
For now we know God has called His best
So when He sends rain again
He is guiding one of His Angels home, and
We have been strong and passed the test
As we pray for strength to the loss of a love one
And as we patiently wait till our turn comes
To finally be among the best for eternal rest
Let God's liquid sunshine and tears,
Wash the sadness and grief away
Because we all know we are not here to stay
But to one day follow that tear stained road
To be in the presence of the Greatest on that glorious day.